BEST OF
BATH

AQVAE · SVLIS

BEST OF
BATH

INDEX

Photographs by **Pitkin Unichrome Ltd** ©
Text by **Tricia Simmonds**
Designed by **Aardvark Design Studio Ltd.**
Published by **Pitkin Unichrome Ltd. (01264) 409200**

© Pitkin Unichrome Ltd, latest edition 1999   2/99

ISBN 1 871004 357 hardcover edition
ISBN 1 871004 071 paperback edition

FRONT COVER:
The Great Bath, used by the Romans as a warm swimming pool and discovered in 1880, was the centrepiece of the baths complex.

Le Great Bath (Grand Bain) utilisé par les Romains en tant que piscine chaude et découverte en 1880, était le point central du complexe des thermes.

Das Große Bad (Great Bath) wurde von den Römern als beheiztes Schwimmbad benutzt und lag im Zentrum der Bäderanlage. Es wurde 1880 entdeckt.

El Great Bath, usado por los Romanos como piscina caliente, fue descubierta en 1880, y es la atracción principal de éste complejo de baños.

BACK COVER:
The interior of the Pump Room designed by Thomas Baldwin.

Intérieur de la Pump Room édifiée par Thomas Baldwin.

Innenansicht des Pump Room, der von Thomas Baldwin entworfen wurde.

El interior de la "Pump Room", donde se puede beber el agua de Bath, diseñada por Thomas Baldwin.

PICTURE OPPOSITE:
Two of Bath's jewels set in stone – Royal Crescent and The Circus

Deux des joyaux architecturaux en pierre de Bath - le Royal Crescent et le Circus.

Zwei architektonische Kostbarkeiten - The Royal Crescent und The Circus.

Dos de las joyas de Bath talladas en piedra - Royal Crescent y The Circus.

PICTURE TITLE PAGE:
The Royal Crescent, described as the finest in Europe, consists of a sweeping arc of 30 houses standing behind a flourish of 114 columns.

Le Royal Crescent, décrit comme le plus beau d'Europe, est un édifice élégant en arc de cercle composé de 30 maisons derrière 114 splendides colonnes.

The Royal Crescent, das als das feinste Gebäude seiner Art in Europa beschrieben wurde, besteht aus dem geschwungenen Halbmond einer Häuserreihe von 30 Häusern hinter einem Bogen von 114 Säulen.

El Royal Crescent, descrito como el más elegante de Europa, consiste en un majestuoso arco de 30 casas erguidas detrás de un despliegue de 114 columnas.

INTRODUCTION

At the heart of Bath lies the source of its name and fame – the mysterious hot mineral water springs. The surrounding historical, cultural and architectural heritage has been left by those who came to wonder, worship, swallow or wallow in its waters.

Legends of the healing powers of the water stretch back to the tale of Prince Bladud, a leper who was banished from court. Forced to work as a swineherd, he noticed that any pig with a skin disease who wallowed in the warm muddy spring waters was cured. He followed their example, became healed and was accepted back into high society. When Bladud in turn became king, he is said to have shown his gratitude by building a bath around the healing spring, lending his name to the city from which Bath is derived.

The Pump Room and Roman Museum together form the font and focus of Bath. Water was bubbling from the ground at this spot when Iron Age Celts hailed the spring sacred and worshipped the god Sul here.

Water at a rate of a quarter of a million gallons a day at a temperature of 117 degrees F, 46.5 degrees C., wells up from the ground. Each droplet started off as a raindrop that fell ten thousand or more years ago on the nearby Mendip Hills. It has been on a fantastic journey, trickling through the rock, surging along huge underground gorges and rivers before being forced up from a depth of 2½ to 3 miles from the earth's hot core to emerge here. Bath's springs are the hottest in Britain.

After invading Britain in AD43, the Romans investigated the steaming swampy spot in the Avon valley that was so revered by the locals.

With Roman efficiency and engineering ingenuity, in the space of 30-40 years they had drained the marsh, contained the water, and built a temple and Britain's first health hydro for restorative and pleasurable purposes. They called their city Aquae Sulis (Sul's Waters) and dedicated their temple to Sulis Minerva, their own goddess of healing.

The stone head of Sul (the Gorgon's head) which adorned the outside of the temple is on display, as is a life-sized gilded bronze head of the goddess Minerva which would have stood inside the temple.

The Romans controlled the flow of waters by building a reservoir (lined with lead mined from the nearby Mendip Hills), a drain and culvert. The overflow of water can be seen today tumbling through the Roman arch on a trilith of stones.

The Baths grew from the first century AD into the vast sophisticated complex that existed into the early years of the fifth century. Alterations and improvements made its development a continuous process. Its paying customers enjoyed heated rooms, saunas, a 'whirlpool', Turkish baths, exercise rooms, hot cubicles, treatment rooms, plunge pools and swimming pools. The centrepiece and most impressive feature of all is the Great Bath, discovered by the Victorians in the 1860s. In the space of 20 years, surrounding property was bought, overlying buildings pulled down and the site excavated so that the public could visit and view the exciting discovery.

At the site of the sacred spring and reservoir, the Romans threw offerings into the water for good luck. These include silver, bronze and pewter cups, plates,

dishes and an oil lamp; carved gemstones and earrings, coins and a selection of lead curses. Monuments to the dead and stone coffins that have been unearthed show that customers travelled from far and wide from Britain and Gaul to visit the spa.

When the Romans left Britain in AD410, the natives lacked the necessary expertise to cope with the problems of silting and flooding. The site rapidly returned to what it was four centuries before – a marsh – and masonry sunk and collapsed into it. Although most of the Roman Baths stayed hidden for centuries, the principal hot spring still gushed and monks ran a healing centre around what remained.

The Abbey site in Bath has been in continuous use for Christian worship since AD676. Edgar, the first King of all England, was crowned in the Saxon Abbey and all coronations since then have been based on that original ceremony. A bishop's dream led to the building of the Abbey that we see today. Bishop Oliver King had a dream in which he saw angels going up and down ladders reaching to heaven. He interpreted this as a sign that he should rebuild the previous ruined building. Work started in 1499. Two master masons, Robert and William Vertue, promised the Bishop "the finest vault in England". The Abbey's fan

vaulted ceiling is indeed its most impressive feature. Building work progressed in a series of stops and stages over the centuries. In the 16th century, Queen Elizabeth I visited Bath and was so shocked by the incomplete Abbey that she ordered collections to be made throughout the land for seven years to fund building work. Bishop Montague took up the restoration challenge in the following century. His tomb is on the north side nave of the Abbey. Hundreds of memorial plaques were added to the walls in the 18th and 19th centuries. The Victorians added

pinnacles, flying buttresses and the nave's stone fan vaulting as mason Vertue originally planned it 350 years earlier.

The Abbey, called the "lantern of the west" as it features more window than wall, is regarded as an outstanding example of Perpendicular English Gothic architecture, and is one of the last great churches built in this style. Its west front symbolically depicts Bishop Oliver King's dream of ladders reaching to heaven with falling and rising angels.

Like the angels on the ladders, Bath's fortunes have risen and fallen over the

centuries. At the beginning of the 18th century, Bath was described ... "Tis a Valley of Pleasure yet a sink of Iniquity. Nor is any intrigues or Debauch Acted in London, but is Mimick'd here." But then came the turning point – Bath's revival and respectability in its Georgian heyday.

Three men transformed the city – Richard 'Beau' Nash, a gambler; Ralph Allen, an entrepreneur and John Wood, an architect. The first provided social tone, the second the stone and the third the classic style that set the standard for the developing city.

Beau Nash was the uncrowned king of the city who set the social, dress and etiquette standards for Georgian Bath. The Pump Room, designed by Thomas Baldwin, is where Beau was Master of Ceremonies and his statue stands where he once presided. To this elegant room, fashionable society came to drink the waters.

Ralph Allen, born 1693, bought the quarries on Combe Down and built Prior Park, the finest and grandest Palladian style mansion in Britain, as a showpiece to advertise the qualities of the stone. The honey-coloured oolitic limestone from Allen's quarries has been shaped into architectural masterpieces which make Georgian Bath unique in Europe.

Prior Park, begun in 1734, was designed by John Wood – the third man to make a great contribution to the city during that era. He came to Bath in 1727 and sought to resurrect the splendour of a Roman city. Queen Square was his first major project, begun in 1729. It was planned to resemble a palace. The Circus, begun in 1754, is considered his finest design. His son, another John, carried on the family expertise with the design of Royal Crescent, a sweeping arc of 30 houses. Its hilltop position gives an unrivalled view over the city. The Assembly Rooms in Bennett Street, also by young John, were the social centre of late Georgian bath where the fashionable flocked to dine and dance, gossip and gamble, to flirt and flaunt their finery. The Assembly Rooms were in continuous use, from serving 2,000 people for breakfasts to grand evening balls. Johann Strauss, Liszt, Rubinstein and Charles Dickens were among the many who performed there. Wealthy traders in the city meanwhile had a rival setting for their own gatherings – the sumptuous Banqueting Hall in the Guildhall, described as one of the finest rooms in Adam style in Europe.

Pulteney Bridge was designed by Robert Adam in 1771 following a competition among architects. It is the only bridge in England with shops on both sides.

Bath became home to the famous, including Louis Napoleon, later Napoleon III; Mrs Maria Fitzherbert, who was secretly married to the Prince of Wales, later King George IV; Lady Hamilton, mistress to Lord Nelson; Jane Austen, Dr David Livingstone the missionary and explorer, Lord Clive of India, Thomas Gainsborough the painter, and William Pitt MP and Prime Minister.

While many came to Bath in its heyday

for the social cachet, some came desperate for a cure from the waters. The Royal Mineral Water Hospital – built by John Wood, using stone supplied by Ralph Allen's quarries and financed by money collected from the visitors by Beau Nash – was supported by Bath's leading physician Dr William Oliver. He invented the Bath Oliver biscuit as an antidote to rich food. It was claimed the waters would cure "gout, rheumatism, palsies, convulsions, lameness, colic, consumption, asthma, jaundice, the itch, scab, leprosy, scrofula, epilepsies, diseases of the eyes, deafness, noise in the ears, palpitations of the heart, sharpness of urine, wounds, ulcers, piles and infertility". A guide to how patients fared after treatment at the hospital in the years 1742-1769 lists: Cured 1,853; Much Better 2,773; Incurable 355, Improper 773, Irregular 78; Dead 169.

Bath today is regarded as one of the loveliest cities in the world and is one of the top tourist attractions in Britain. Its natural and man-made wonders are enhanced by the seasons, whether decked in snow or flowers. Whatever the mood, angle or era, this book is designed to show Bath at its best.

C'est au coeur de Bath que l'on trouve l'origine de son nom et de sa réputation - ses eaux minérales thermales empruntes de mystère. L'héritage historique, culturel et architectural environnant a été légué par ceux qui sont venus s'émerveiller, faire leurs dévotions, boire cette eau ou s'y baigner.

Les légendes sur les pouvoirs de guérison de cette eau remontent au conte du Prince Bladud, un lépreux banni de la Cour. Forcé à travailler comme porcher, il remarqua que tous les porcs souffrant d'une maladie affectant leur peau étaient guéris lorsqu'ils se baignaient dans ces sources chaudes et boueuses. Il suivit leur exemple, fut guéri lui aussi et fut de nouveau accepté par la haute société. Et l'on raconte que lorsque Bladud devint roi à son tour, il montra sa gratitude en faisant construire des bains autour de cette source

de guérison, donnant ainsi son nom à la ville de Bath.

La Salle des pompes (Pump Room) et le Musée des bains romains (Roman Baths Museum) constituent le fondement et le centre d'intérêt de Bath. L'eau sortait du sol en bouillonnant à cet endroit lorsque les Celtes de l'âge de fer faisaient les louanges de cette source sacrée et adoraient leur dieu Sul.

Aujourd'hui, l'eau jaillit du sol à un débit de 4,5 millions de litres par jour et à une température de 46,5°C. Chaque goutelette était à l'origine une goutte de pluie qui est tombée il y a dix mille ans ou plus sur les collines Mendip Hills avoisinantes. Les eaux thermales de Bath sont les plus chaudes de Grande-Bretagne.

Après avoir envahi la Grande-Bretagne en l'an 43 ap J.-C., les Romains ont examiné cet endroit baigné de vapeurs et marécageux dans la vallée d'Avon que les habitants vénéraient tant.

Grâce à leur efficacité et à leur ingéniosité technique, en l'espace de 30-40 ans les Romains ont drainé le marécage, contenu l'eau et construit un temple ainsi que les premières thermes de Grande-Bretagne, lieu de guérison et de loisir. Ils appelèrent leur ville Aquae Sulis (Les Eaux de Sul) et dédièrent leur temple à Sulis Minerva, leur déesse de la guérison.

Les thermes ont connu une expansion dès le premier siècle

ap J.-C. pour devenir le grand complexe sophistiqué qui existait au début du cinquième siècle. Les changements et améliorations qui y ont été apportés

permirent leur développement continu.

Lorsque les Romains quittèrent la Grande-Bretagne en l'an 410 ap J.-C., les habitants de la ville n'avaient ni le savoir-faire ni l'expérience nécessaires pour surmonter les problèmes d'envasement et d'inondations. Le site retourna à l'état dans lequel il était quatres siècles auparavant - un marécage - et la maçonnerie s'enfonça puis s'effondra. Bien que la plupart des bains romains soient restés dans cet état pendant des siècles, la source thermale principale jaillissait toujours avec force et des moines établirent alors un centre de guérison autour des vestiges.

Le site de l'Abbaye de Bath est un lieu de culte chrétien depuis 676. Edgar, le premier roi d'Angleterre, fut couronné dans l'Abbaye saxonne (Saxon Abbey) et tous les couronnements qui suivirent ont été basés sur cette cérémonie. Le rêve d'un évêque devint réalité lorsque l'Abbaye fut construite, telle que nous la connaissons aujourd'hui. En effet, l'évêque Oliver King fit un rêve dans lequel des anges montaient et descendaient des échelles conduisant au paradis et l'interpréta comme un signe pour faire reconstruire l'ancien bâtiment en ruines. Les travaux commencèrent en 1499; deux maîtres-maçons, Robert et William Vertue promirent à l'évêque "la plus belle voûte d'Angleterre". Et c'est pour cette raison que la voûte en éventail de cette abbaye est l'une de ses caractéristiques les plus impressionnantes. Les travaux de construction se firent en plusieurs stades en raison de nombreuses interruptions au fil des siècles.

Cette Abbaye, appelée la "lanterne de l'ouest", car elle comporte plus de fenêtres que de murs, est considérée comme un exemple remarquable d'architecture gothique anglaise de style perpendiculaire et est l'une des dernières églises abbatiales grandioses bâties dans ce style. Sa façade orientée vers l'ouest illustre de façon symbolique le rêve de l'évêque Oliver King, puisqu'elle est ornée d'échelles conduisant au paradis avec des anges montant et descendant.

Tout comme les anges sur ces échelles, le sort de Bath a connu des hauts et des bas au fil des siècles. Au début du 18ème siècle, Bath était décrite en ces termes "C'est une vallée de plaisir, mais un cloaque de vices. Les intrigues et les actes de débauche ne sont pas commis à Londres, mais imités ici." Puis elle connut une période décisive - la renaissance de Bath et sa respectabilité retrouvée, son âge d'or pendant le règne des quatre rois George.

Trois hommes transformèrent la ville - Richard "Beau" Nash, un joueur, Ralph Allen, un entrepreneur et John Wood, un architecte. Le premier apporta la touche de classe célèbre, le second la pierre et le troisième le style classique qui influença cette ville en développement.

Beau Nash était le roi non couronné de la ville et il établit les normes de la société, les règles vestimentaires et l'étiquette pour la ville de Bath à cette époque. La Salle des Pompes (Pump Room), dessinée par Thomas Baldwin était la salle où Beau fut Maître des Cérémonies, et sa statue se dresse là où il présidait autrefois. La haute société de l'époque venait boire l'eau de source dans cette pièce élégante.

Ralph Allen, né en 1693, acheta les carrières de Combe Down et fit construire Prior Park, le château style palladien le plus beau et le plus majestueux de Grande-Bretagne, comme pièce d'exposition pour faire connaître les qualités de la pierre. Le calcaire oolithique couleur miel des carrières d'Allen a permis de réaliser des chefs-d'oeuvres architecturaux qui donnent à Bath son caractère unique en Europe.

Prior Park, dont la construction commença en 1734, a été dessiné par John Wood - le troisième homme ayant apporté une grande contribution à la ville à cette époque. Il arriva à Bath en 1727 et chercha à recréer la splendeur d'une cité romaine. Queen Square fut son premier grand projet, dont la construction commença en 1729. Le Circus, commencé en 1754 est considéré comme sa plus belle création. Son fils poursuivit le savoir-faire et l'expérience de la famille avec son dessin du Royal Crescent, un édifice élégant en arc de cercle composé de 30 maisons. Les salles de réunions (Assembly Rooms) dans Bennett Street, également dessinées par Wood fils, étaient à l'époque le lieu à Bath où les gens du beau monde venaient dîner et danser, bavarder et jouer, flirter et parader.

Pulteney Bridge a été conçu par Robert Adam en 1771 à la suite d'un concours d'architectes. C'est le seul pont en Angleterre avec des magasins des deux côtés.

Parmi les personnes célèbres ayant choisi de vivre à Bath

ont figuré Louis Napoléon, qui devint Napoléon III, Mme Maria Fitzherbert, épouse secrète du Prince de Galles devenu ensuite le roi George IV, Lady Hamilton, maîtresse de Lord Nelson, Jane Austen, le missionnaire et explorateur Dr. David Livingstone, Lord Clive d'Inde, le peintre Thomas Gainsborough et William Pitt, Membre de la Chambre des Communes et Premier Ministre.

Tandis qu'un grand nombre de personnes étaient attirées par Bath en raison de sa haute société, d'autres venaient dans l'espoir de guérir grâce à sa source thermale. Le Royal Mineral Water Hospital, construction de John Wood faisant appel aux carrières de Ralph Allen et financée par l'argent amassé par Beau Nash grâce aux visiteurs, a reçu le soutien du médecin le plus éminent de Bath, Dr. William Oliver, qui inventa le biscuit Bath Oliver comme antidote contre une alimentation riche.

Aujourd'hui, Bath est considérée comme l'une des plus belles villes du monde et l'une des attractions touristiques les plus prisées en Grande-Bretagne. Ses merveilles naturelles et réalisées par l'homme sont embellies par les saisons, que la ville soit recouverte de neige ou parsemée de fleurs. Quels que soient l'humeur, l'angle sous lequel on admire cette ville ou l'époque qu'elle évoque, le but de ce livre est de faire découvrir Bath dans toute sa beauté.

Den Ausgangs- und Mittelpunkt von Bath bilden das Brunnenhaus und das Museum der römischen Bäder. Die hier in der Eisenzeit aus dem Boden sprudelnde Quelle wurde von den Kelten als heilig erklärt und diente als Kultstätte für den keltischen Gott Sul.

Die Quelle fördert täglich etwa 1137 Hektoliter Wasser mit einer Temperatur von 46,5°C. Jeder Tropfen begann als ein Regentropfen, der vor zehntausend oder mehr Jahren auf die nahegelegenen Mendip Hills fiel. Die Quellen von Bath sind die wärmsten in Großbritannien.

Nach ihrem Einfall in England im Jahr 43 AD untersuchten die Römer die von den Ortsansässigen so verehrte, dampfende, sumpfige Stelle im Avon-Tal.

Mit römischer Gründlichkeit und technischer Genialität hatten sie das Gebiet innerhalb von 30 bis 40 Jahren trockengelegt, die Quelle gefaßt und einen Tempel und die erste Kuranlage Großbritanniens für Stärkungs- und Erholungszwecke gebaut. Die Römer nannten ihre Stadt Aquae Sulis (Suls Wasser) und weihten ihren Tempel der Sulis-Minerva, ihrer eigenen Göttin der Heilung.

Aus diesen ersten Bauten wurden die Bäder auf den bis Anfang des fünften Jahrhunderts vorhandenen riesigen, hochentwickelten Anlagenkomplex ausgebaut, dessen Entwicklung durch Änderungen und Verbesserungen zu einem anhaltenden Prozeß wurde.

Als die Römer 410 AD aus Großbritannien abzogen, fehlte es den Einheimischen an der erforderlichen Fachkenntnis, um mit den Verschlammungs- und Überschwemmungsproblemen fertig zu werden. Die Anlage wurde in kurzer Zeit wieder zu dem, was sie vierhundert Jahr zuvor schon einmal gewesen war, nämlich einem Sumpf. Die Bauten versanken und zerfielen darin. Die meisten der römischen Bäder blieben zwar jahrhundertelang verborgen, die Hauptquelle sprudelte jedoch immer noch. Um die Reste der Bäderanlage unterhielten Mönche ein Heilzentrum.

Das Gelände der Abtei in Bath dient schon seit 676 ohne Unterbrechung als christliche Andachtsstätte. Edgar, der erste König von England, wurde in der angelsächsischen Abtei gekrönt. Diese erste Zeremonie liegt allen seither stattgefundenen Krönungen zu Grunde. Das Abteigebäude, wie wir es heute kennen, geht auf den Traum des Bischofs Oliver King zurück, in dem dieser Engel auf Leitern in den Himmel hinauf-

D en Kern der Stadt Bath bildet der Ursprung ihres Namens und ihrer Berühmtheit - die geheimnisvollen heißen Mineralquellen. Das historische, kulturelle und architektonische Erbe an diesen Quellen geht auf jene zurück, die ihr Wasser bewunderten, verehrten, tranken oder darin badeten.

Die Legenden über die Heilkräfte des Wassers gehen zurück bis auf die Sage vo dem leprakranken Prinz Bladud. Er wurde aufgrund seiner Krankheit vom königlichen Hof verbannt und war gezwungen, als Schweinehirt zu arbeiten. Bei der Arbeit mit den Tieren bemerkte er, daß jedes Schwein mit einer Hauterkrankung, das sich im warmen Schlamm der Quellen suhlte, wieder gesund wurde. Der Prinz folgte diesem Beispiel, wurde geheilt und am Hofe wieder aufgenommen. Es heißt, daß Bladud, als er König wurde, seine Dankbarkeit dadurch zum Ausdruck brachte, daß er um die Heilquelle herum ein Bad bauen ließ. Dadurch erhielt die Stadt, Vorgängerin des heutigen Bath, ihren Namen.

und von dort heruntersteigen sah. Er deutete diesen Traum als ein Zeichen, daß er das bis dahin zerfallene Gebäude wieder aufbauen sollte. Mit der Arbeit wurde 1499 begonnen. Zwei Meistersteinmetzen, Robert und William Vertue, versprachen dem Bischof das "feinste Gewölbe in England". Die Fächergewölbedecke der Abtei ist auch wirklich das beeindruckendste Merkmal des Gebäudes. Die Bauarbeiten wurden in einer Reihe von Unterbrechungen und Bauphasen über Jahrhunderte hinweg fortgesetzt.

Die Abtei wird die "Laterne des Westens" genannt, da sie mehr Fenster- als Wandfläche aufweist, und gilt als ein hervorragendes Beispiel der perpendikularen englischen Gothik. Sie ist eine der letzten großen Kirchen, die in diesem Stil gebaut wurde. An ihrer Westfront befindet sich die symbolische Darstellung von Bishof Oliver Kings Traum von in den Himmel reichenden Leitern mit fallenden und aufsteigenden Engeln.

Das hier abgebildete Auf und Ab zeigte sich auch im Geschick der Stadt Bath. Anfang des 18. Jahrhunderts hieß es von Bath: ..."es ist ein Tal der Freuden und doch ein Sündenpfuhl. Es gibt in London keine Intrige und kein Laster, das hier nicht seinesgleichen hat." Doch dann kam der Wendepunkt - die Renaissance und Angesehenheit der Stadt in ihrer georgianischen Glanzzeit.

Dieser Wandel wurde von drei Männern bewirkt - Richard "Beau" Nash, einem Spieler, Ralph Allen, einem Unternehmer, und John Wood, einem Architekten. Der erste gab den gesellschaftlichen Ton an, der zweite lieferte das Baumaterial und der dritte den klassischen Stil, der die Maßstäbe für die sich entwickelnde Stadt Bath setzte.

Beau Nash war der ungekrönte König der Stadt, der im georgianischen Bath bezüglich Gesellschaft, Kleidung und Etikette tonangebend war. Im von Thomas Baldwin entworfenen Brunnenhaus war Beau Zeremonienmeister, seine Statue steht heute dort, wo er präsidierte. In diesen eleganten Raum kamen die Vornehmen der britischen Gesellschaft zur Trinkkur.

Ralph Allen, geboren 1693, kaufte die Steinbrüche am Combe Down und baute Prior Park, das feinste und großartigste Herrenhaus im Palladin-Stil. Prior Park diente zur Werbung für die Qualitäten des Steins. Der honigfarbene oolithische Kalkstein aus Allens Steinbrüchen wurde zu architektonischen Meisterstücken geformt, aufgrund derer das georgianische Bath europaweit einzigartig ist.

Entworfen wurde Prior Park, mit dessen Bau 1734 begonnen wurde, von John Wood, dem dritten Mann, der in dieser Ära einen bedeutenden Beitrag zur Stadt leistete. Er kam 1727 nach Bath und beabsichtigte, die Pracht einer römischen Stadt wiederherzustellen. Queen Square war sein erstes größeres Projekt, das 1729 begonnen wurde. Der "Circus", mit dessen Bau 1754 begonnen wurde, gilt als sein bester Entwurf. Sein Sohn, ebenfalls John Wood, führte die berufliche Tradition seiner Familie mit der Planung von Royal Crescent, einem aus 30 Häusern bestehenden Gebäudebogen, fort. Er entwarf auch die Assembly Rooms in Bennett Street, die den gesellschaftlichen Mittelpunkt des spätgeorgianischen Bath bildeten. Hier trafen sich die Vornehmen in Scharen zum Essen und Tanzen, Klatschen und Spielen, Flirten und Aufsehenerregen.

Pulteney Bridge wurde 1771 von Robert Adam auf einen Wettbewerb unter Architekten hin entworfen. Sie ist die einzige Brücke in England mit Läden auf beiden Seiten.

Viele kamen in der Glanzzeit der Stadt aufgrund ihres gesellschaftlichen Gütesiegels nach Bath, andere, weil sie verzweifelt auf eine Heilung durch ihre Quellen hofften. Das Royal Mineral Water Hospital - von John Wood mit Steinen aus Ralph Allens Steinbrüchen gebaut und mit von Beau Nash bei den Besuchern der Stadt gesammeltem Geld finanziert - hatte die Unterstützung des führenden Arztes von Bath, Dr. William Oliver. Er erfand das Bath Oliver Keks als ein Gegenmittel gegen schwere, üppige Speisen.

Bath gilt heute als eine der reizendsten Städte der Welt und eine der Spitzenattraktionen für Touristen in Großbritannien. Die natürlichen und die von Menschenhand geschaffenen Wunder der Stadt sind in jeder Jahreszeit - schneebedeckt oder in Blüten gehüllt - sehenswert. Dieses Heft soll Bath von seiner besten Seite zeigen, ganz gleich, welche Stimmung, Blickwinkel und Zeitalter betrachtet werden.

En el corazón de Bath yace la fuente de su nombre y fama - las misteriosas fuentes termales. El patrimonio histórico, cultural y arquitectónico de sus alrededores es la huella de aquéllos que vinieron a admirar, venerar, probar o sumirse en sus aguas.

Las leyendas de los poderes curativos de sus aguas se remontan a la época del Príncipe Bladud, un leproso desterrado de la corte. Al verse obligado a trabajar como porquero, noto que aquellos animales con enfermedades de piel que se sumergían en las cálidas y fangosas aguas del manantial se curaban. Siguió ese ejemplo, curándose y siendo acceptado de nuevo en la alta sociedad. Cuando Bladud fue coronado rey, se dice que mostro su gratitud construyendo un baño alrededor del manantial de poderes curativos, prestando su nombre a la ciudad de donde se deriva el nombre de Bath ("Baño").

El Museo de la Sala de Bombeo y los Baños Romanos forman la pila y foco de Bath. Agua brotaba de la tierra en ese lugar cuando los Céltas de la Edad de Hierro aclamaban el manantial sagrado y adoraban aqui al dios Sul.

El agua mana de la tierra a un caudal de un cuarto de millón de galones al día a una temperatura de 117 grados Fahrenheit, 46,5°C. Cada gotita empezó como una gota de lluvia que cayó hace más de diez mil millones de años en las cercanas colinas de Mendip. Los manantiales de Bath son los más calientes de Gran Bretaña.

Después de invadir Gran Bretaña en AD43, los Romanos investigaron éste vaporoso y pantanoso lugar en el valle de Avon, el cual era muy venerado por los habitantes de alrededor.

Con eficacia e ingenuidad en ingeniería Romana, en el transcurso de 30-40 años habían vaciado el pantano, contenido sus aguas, construido un templo y el primer balneario reconstituyente y recreativo de Gran Bretaña. Nombraron su ciudad Aqua Sulis (Agua de Sul) y dedicaron su tempo a Sulis Minerva, su diosa de poderes curativos.

A partir del primer siglo AD, los Baños se convirtieron en un extenso y sofisticado complejo y continuó operando hasta principios del siglo V. Alteraciones y amejoramientos hicieron que su desarrollo sea un proceso contínuo.

Cuando los Romanos dejaron Gran Bretaña en AD410, los nativos carecían de suficiente conocimiento para abarcar con problemas de obstrucciones debido a sedimentos e inundaciones. El yacimiento se convirtió rápidamente en lo que había sido hace cuatro siglos - un pantano - y la mampostería se hundió y derrumbó en el pantano. A pesar de que la mayor parte de los Baños Romanos quedaron escondidos durante siglos, el principal manantial caliente seguía borbotando, y los monjes manejaron un centro curativo entorno a lo que quedaba.

El emplazamiento de la Abadía en Bath fue usado como lugar de adoración Cristiana desde 676. Edgar, el primer Rey de toda Inglaterra, fue coronado en la Abadía de Saxon y desde entonces todas las coronaciones se basan en ésa primera ceremonia. Un sueño de un Obispo fue la inspiración para la construcción de la Abadía que podemos ver hoy. El Obispo Oliver King tuvo un sueño en el cual vió ángeles subiendo y bajando escaleras que alcanzaban al cielo. Interpreto este sueño como una llamada para reconstruir el edificio que yacía en ruinas. Las obras comenzaron en 1499. Robert y William Vertue, dos maestros en construcciones, prometieron al Obispo "la bóveda más bella de Inglaterra". El raso de la bóveda en forma de abanico es sin duda la característica más impresionante de la Abadía.

Los trabajos de obra progresaron a tropezones y en varias etapas a través de los siglos.

La Abadía, llamada "la linterna del Oeste" al caracterizar más ventanas que paredes, es considerada como un ejemplar único de arquitectura Gótica Perpendicular Inglesa, y es una de las últimas iglesias importantes construidas en éste estilo. Su fachada al Oeste simboliza el sueño del Obispo Oliver King con escaleras alcanzando al cielo con ángeles cayendose y subiendo.

Como los ángeles en las escaleras, las fortunas de Bath crecieron y disminuyeron a través de los siglos. Al principio del siglo XVIII, se describía Bath como... "Un valle de placer sin embargo una sentina. Cualquier acto de corrupción o intriga que ocurra en Londres se copia aqui". Pero entonces vino un cambio decisivo - el resurgimiento y respetabilidad de Bath durante su apogeo a principios del siglo diez y nueve.

Tres personas transformaron la ciudad - Richard "Beau" Nash, un jugador, Ralph Allen, un hombre de negocios y John Wood, un arquitecto. El primero proporciono el tono social, el segundo la piedra y el tercero el estilo clásico que marco el tono de la ciudad en desarrollo.

Beau Nash fue el rey sin corona de la ciudad que marco el nivel social, la moda y etiqueta de la ciudad de Bath a principio del siglo diez y nueve. La Sala de Bombeo, diseñada por Thomas Paldwin, es donde Beau fue Maestro de Ceremonias y su estátua se alza donde solía presidir. A ésta elegante sala, gente famosa de sociedad venía a beber sus aguas.

Ralph Allen, nacido en 1693, adquirió la cantera de Combe Down y contruyó Prior Park, la mansión más refinada y resplendorosa de estilo Paladesco en Gran Bretaña, esta mansión fue erguida para promulgar las calidades de la piedra. La piedra caliza de color miel procedente de la cantera de Allen ha sido moldeada en obras maestras de arquitectura que hace la ciudad de Bath a principios del siglo diez y nueve única en Europa.

Las obras de Prior Park, comenzaron en 1734, y fue diseñada por John Wood - el tercer hombre que contribuyó enormemente en el desarrollo de la ciudad durante ésta época. Se installo en Bath en 1727 y busco en resucitar el esplendor de la ciudad Romana. Queen Square fue su primer proyecto importante, cuyas obras comenzaron en 1729. Las obras del Circus, comenzaron en 1754, y es considerado como su mejor diseño. Su hijo, otro John, continuó la tradición de su familia con el diseño del Royal Crescent, un majestuoso arco de 30 casas. El Assembly Rooms en Bennett Street, diseñado también por el joven John, fueron el foco social de Bath a finales de la época Georgiana, donde la gente famosa iba a cenar y a bailar, a cotillear y aventurar en el juego, a coquetear y a lucir sus galas.

Pulteney Bridge fue diseñado por Robert Adam en 1771 después de haber ganado un concurso entre arquitectos. Es el único puente en Inglaterra que tiene tiendas en ambos lados.

Bath fue el hogar de muchos personajes famosos, entre ellos Luis Napoleón, más tarde Napoleón III; Sra María Fitzherbert, quien estaba casada secretamente al Príncipe de Gales, quien fue coronado mas tarde Rey Jorge IV, Lady Hamilton, amante de Lord Nelson; Jane Austen; el misionario y explorador Dr David Livingstone, Lord Clive de India, el pintor Thomas Gainsborough, y el Primer Ministro William Pitt M.P.

Mientrás que muchos venían a Bath

durante su apogeo por su cachet social, algunos vinieron a sus agua desesperados en busca de una cura. El Hospital Royal Mineral Water - construido por John Wood, utilizando piedras procedentes de la cantera de Ralph Allen y financiado con dinero recaudado a través de visitantes por Beau Nash - fue apoyado por el Dr William Oliver, el cirujano mas importante de Bath, que inventó la galleta Bath Oliver, el antidoto perfecto a comidas pesadas.

Hoy en día Bath es considerada una de las ciudades más bonitas del mundo y una de las atracciones turísticas más importantes de Gran Bretaña. Sus maravillas naturales y aquellas hecha por la mano del hombre se embellezen con las estaciones, este cubierta con nieve o con flores. Sea cual sea su disposición, punto de vista o época, éste libro esta diseñado a mostrarle Bath en su esplendor.

THE BATHS

The Great Bath, used by the Romans as a warm swimming pool and discovered in 1880, was the centrepiece of the baths complex. Several tons of lead sheeting which came from the Mendip Hills during the Roman period line the floor.

■Le Great Bath (Grand Bain) utilisé par les Romains en tant que piscine chaude et découverte en 1880, était le point central du complexe des thermes. Plusieurs tonnes de feuilles de plomb provenant des collines Mendip Hills du temps des Romains supportent le plancher.

■Das Große Bad (Great Bath) wurde von den Römern als beheiztes Schwimmbad benutzt und lag im Zentrum der Bäderanlage. Es wurde 1880 entdeckt. Sein Boden ist mit mehreren Tonnen Blei aus den Mendip Hills ausgekleidet.

■El Great Bath, usado por los Romanos como piscina caliente, fue descubierta en 1880, y es la atracción principal de éste complejo de baños. Varias toneladas de laminado de plomo traídas desde las colinas de Mendip durante el periódo Romano aliñan el suelo.

The King's Bath lies over the sacred spring and reservoir.

■Le King's Bath (Bain du Roi) est situé au-dessus de la source sacrée et du réservoir.

■Das Königsbad (King's Bath) liegt über der heiligen Quelle und dem Reservoir.

■El King's Bath esta situado más arriba del manantial y del embalse subterráneo natural sagrado.

The overflow of the hot spring tumbles through a Roman arch on a trilith of stones. The water contains so much iron that it has stained the stone.

■ *Le trop-plein de la source thermale s'écoule avec force par une arche romaine sur un trilithe en pierre. L'eau contient tellement de fer qu'elle a tâché la pierre.*

■ *Das am Überlauf der heißen Quelle heraussprudelnde Wasser läuft durch einen römischen Bogen auf Trilithen. Das Wasser enthält so viel Eisen, daß es den Stein verfärbt hat.*

■ *La cañería de desagüe del manantial caliente reboza en un arco Romano sobre un conjunto de piedras. El agua contiene tanto plomo que ha teñido la piedra.*

The Great Bath, around 26 by 13 metres, originally had a barrel-vaulted roof. Alcoves along the sides of the Great bath allowed onlookers to sit, gossip and relax away from the splashes of the bathers.

■ *Le Grand Bain, qui mesure environ 26 mètres sur 13, avait à l'origine une voûte en forme de berceau. Les alcôves sur les côtés permettaient aux personnes se contentant de regarder, de s'assoeir, bavarder et se détendre sans être éclaboussées par les baigneurs.*

■ *Das Große Bad (ca. 26 m lang und 13 m breit) hatte ursprünglich ein Tonnengewölbedach. In Nischen an den Seiten des Bads konnten Zuschauer ungestört sitzen, sich unterhalten und entspannen.*

■ *El Great Bath, con unas dimensiones aproximadas de 26 metros por 13 metros, originalmente tubo un tejado con bóveda de cañón. Nichos a los largo de los costados del Great Bath permitía que espectadores se sentasen, cotilleasen y se relajasen fuera del alcanze de los chapoteos de los bañistas.*

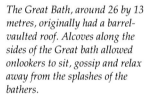

The hypocaust rooms were heated by hot air flowing under the floor. Air was heated by furnaces outside the rooms and drawn by ducted flue.

■ *Les salles des hypocaustes étaient chauffées par un écoulement d'air chaud dans le sol. L'air était chauffé par des fourneaux en dehors de ces salles puis aspiré par des conduites.*

■ *Die hypokaustischen Räume wurden mit unter dem Fußboden strömender heißer Luft beheizt. Die Luft wurde außerhalb der Räume von Öfen erwärmt und in Heizkanälen angesaugt.*

■ *Estas salas con suelos de madera se calentaban a través de aire caliente que circulaba a través del suelo. El aire se calentaba en hornos situados fuera de las salas y se extraía por medio de tubos canalizados.*

The spring water that feeds the baths is a constant 46.5 degrees C. The steam rising from the water at dawn adds an aura of mystery to the scene.

■*L'eau de source qui alimente les thermes est à une température constante de 46,5°C. La vapeur s'élevant au-dessus de l'eau à l'aube ajoute une aura de mystère à la scène.*

■*Das Quellwasser, aus dem die Bäder gespeist werden, hat eine konstante Temperatur von 46,5 Grad Celsius. Der aufsteigende Dampf verleiht der Szene eine geheimnisvolle Atmosphäre.*

■*El manantial de agua que alimenta los baños esta a una temperatura constante de 46.5°C. El vapor que surge de las aguas al amanecer añade una emanación misteriosa a la escena.*

The treasured exhibit of the Roman Baths museum is the life-sized gilded bronze head of the goddess Minerva which would have adorned the Roman temple.

■*La pièce d'extrême valeur exposée au Musée des bains romains est la tête, grandeur nature, en bronze doré de la déesse Minerva qui ornait le temple Romain.*

■*Das kostbarste Stück im Museum der römischen Bäder (Roman Baths Museum) ist der lebensgroße, vergoldete Bronzekopf der Göttin Minverva aus dem römischen Tempel.*

■*La pieza más valiosa que posee el museo de los Roman Baths es la cabeza dorada de bronce de la diosa Minerva la cual adornaba el templo Romano.*

Through the arch at the King's Bath, the Romans threw their offerings to the gods at the site of the sacred spring.

■Les Romains jetaient leurs offrandes aux dieux, là où se trouvait la source sacrée, à travers l'arche du Bain du Roi.

■Durch den Bogen am Königsbad warfen die Römer ihre Opfergaben für die Götter an der heiligen Quelle.

■Pasándo a través del arco en el King's Bath, los Romanos arrojaban sus ofrendas a los dioses en el lugar del manantial sagrado.

Upon the sacrificial altar in front of the Roman temple, offerings to the gods were placed and the entrails of animals examined to foretell the future.

■Les offrandes faites aux dieux et les entrailles des animaux examinées pour prédire l'avenir étaient placées sur l'autel des sacrifices, situé en face du temple Romain.

■Auf den Opferaltar vor dem römischen Tempel wurden Opfer für die Götter gelegt und die Eingeweide von Tieren untersucht, um daraus die Zukunft zu prophezeien.

■En el altar de sacrificio, delante del templo Romano, colocaban las ofrendas a los dioses y entrañas de animales se examinaban para presagiar el futuro.

Hot water flows directly from the Roman reservoir into the Great Bath through lead conduits.

■Les eaux chaudes s'écoulaient directement du réservoir Romain dans le Grand Bain par des conduites en plomb.

■Heißes Wasser fließt in Bleirohren direkt aus dem römischen Reservoir in das Große Bad.

■A través de conductos de plomo, el agua caliente corría directamente desde el embalse subterráneo natural hasta el Great Bath a través de conductos de plomo.

21

The Circular Bath.

■ *Le Circular Bath (Bain Circulaire).*

■ *Das runde Bad (Circular Bath).*

■ *El Baño Circular.*

King Bladud lent his name to the city from which Bath is derived. Legend tells that on noticing how the warm muddy waters of the area cured his pigs of skin diseases, he followed their example and cured himself of leprosy. He then built a bath around the healing spring.

■ *Le roi Bladud a donné son nom à la cité dont Bath dérive. La légende raconte que remarquant que les eaux chaudes et boueuses de cet endroit guérissaient ses porcs souffrant de maladies affectant leur peau, il suivit leur exemple et fut guéri de sa lèpre. Il fit alors construire des bains autour de cette source de guérison.*

■ *Der Name der Stadt Bath geht auf King Bladud zurück. Eine Legende erzählt, daß er bemerkte, daß das warme, schlammige Wasser an dieser Stelle die Hautkrankheiten seiner Schweine heilte. Er folgte dem Beispiel der Tiere und heilte sich so von Lepra. Später faßte er die Heilquelle dann in ein Bad.*

The Iron-Age Celts worshipped the god Sul and the powerful and enigmatic stone-carved Gorgon's Head, or Head of Sul, once adorned Bath's Roman Temple.

■ *Les Celtes de l'Age de Fer adoraient le dieu Sul, et la tête impressionnante et énigmatique de Gordon, ou tête de Sul, sculptée dans la pierre, ornait autrefois le temple romain de Bath.*

■ *Die Kelten der Eisenzeit verehrten den Gott Sul. Der mächtige, rätselhafte steinerne Gorgonenkopf oder Kopf des Sul schmückte den römischen Tempel.*

■ *Los Céltas de la Edad de Hierro adoraban al dios Sul y la poderosa y enigmática Cabeza de Gordon carvada en piedra, o la Cabeza de Sul, adornó antiguamente el Templo Romano de Bath.*

■ *El Rey Bladud presto su nombre a la ciudad desde dónde se deriva el nombre de Bath. La leyenda dice que cuando él se apercibió que las cálidas y fangosas aguas de la zona curaban a sus cerdos de enfermedades de la piel, el hizo lo mismo y se curó también de lepra. Fue entoncés, cuando él mandó construir un baño alrededor del manantial curativo.*

BEAU NASH'S GEORGIAN BATH

The three curved crescents of The Circus form a circle nearly 100 metres in diameter. Dr David Livingstone the explorer, Lord Clive of India, Thomas Gainsborough the painter and William Pitt, MP and Prime Minister once lived there.

■Les trois rues en arc de cercle du Circus forment un cercle de près de 100 mètres de diamètre. L'explorateur Dr. David Livingstone, Lord Clive d'Inde, le peintre Thomas Gainsborough et William Pitt, Membre de la Chambre des Communes et Premier Ministre, ont tous vécu là.

■Die drei halbmondförmigen Gebäudebogen des The Circus bilden einen Kreis mit einem Durchmesser von fast 100 m. Der Forscher Dr. David Livingston, Lord Clive von Indien, der Maler Thomas Gainsborough und William Pitt, Parlamentsmitglied und Premierminister, wohnten hier.

■Las tres calles curvadas en forma de arco del Circus forman un círculo de más de 100 metros en diámetro. El explorador Dr David Livingstone, Lord Clive de las Indias, el pintor Thomas Gainsborough y el Miembro de Parlamento y Primer Ministro William Pitt vivieron una vez aquí.

The Circus, designed by John Wood the elder in 1754, featuring stone carved acorn decoration.

■Le Circus, dessiné par John Wood père en 1754, avec des décorations sculptées représentant des glands.

■The Circus, von John Wood dem Älteren 1754 entworfen, mit gemeißelter Eichelverzierung.

■El Circus, diseñado por John Wood el mayor en 1754, se caracteriza por sus piedras carvadas en forma de bellotas.

Lansdown Crescent, dating from 1789, has been described as a 'hillside frill'. It offers a superb view over Bath.

■Lansdown Crescent, datant de 1789, a été décrit comme une "fioriture de colline". Il offre une vue superbe sur Bath.

■Lansdown Crescent aus dem Jahr 1789 wurde einmal als eine "Rüsche am Hang" bezeichnet. Von hier hat man einen wunderbaren Blick auf Bath.

■Lansdown Crescent, data de 1789, se ha descrito como una "ladera adornada". Ofrece una panorámica magnífica de Bath.

The north front of the Pump Room, designed by Thomas Baldwin, bears the Greek inscription Water is Best.

■La façade nord de la Salle des pompes, dessinée par Thomas Baldwin, porte l'inscription grecque "L'eau est ce qu'il y a de meilleur".

■Die griechische Inschrift an der von Thomas Baldwin entworfenen Nordfront der Trinkhalle bedeutet: "Wasser ist am besten".

■La fachada al Norte de la Sala de Bombeo, diseñada por Thomas Baldwin, lleva la inscripción Griega "Agua es Mejor".

The 18th century Assembly Rooms – a Ballroom, the Octagon card room, the Long Card room and Tea Room. A corporate syndicate financed the £20,000 venture whose success depended on Bath's continuing social popularity.

■ *Les Salles de réunion (Assembly Rooms) - une salle de bal, la salle des cartes Octagon, la Long Card Room et la Tea Room. Un syndicat d'entreprise finança ce projet de £20.000 dont le succès dépendait de la popularité continue de Bath auprès de la haute société.*

■ *Die Assembly Rooms aus dem 18. Jahrhundert bestehen aus einem Ballsaal, dem Oktagon-Kartenzimmer, dem Langen Kartenzimmer und dem Teesaal. Das 60.000-Mark-Unternehmen, dessen Erfolg von der anhaltenden gesellschaftlichen Beliebtheit von Bath abhing, wurde von einem Konsortium finanziert.*

■ *El Assembly Rooms del siglo XVIII - con su sala de baile, sala Octágona de juego de barajas, la sala de Long Card y la Sala de Té. Un sindicato colectivo financió éste proyecto por un valor de £20,000 en cuyo éxito dependía la sobrevivencia de Bath como centro social de moda.*

Cavendish Crescent, dating from the early 19th century, was the work of John Finch.

■ *Cavendish Crescent, datant du début du 19ème siècle, est l'oeuvre de John Pinch.*

■ *Cavendish Crescent wurde Anfang des 19. Jahrhunderts von John Pinch erbaut.*

■ *Cavendish Crescent, de principios del siglo XIX, fue la obra de John Pinch.*

Above Cavendish Crescent lies Somerset Place, dating from the late 18th century and designed by John Eveleigh.

■ *Après Cavendish Square, on arrive à Somerset Place, datant de la fin du 18ème siècle et dessiné par John Eveleigh.*

■ *Oberhalb von Cavendish Crescent liegt Somerset Place, das Ende des 18. Jahrhunderts nach einem Entwurf von John Eveleigh erbaut wurde.*

■ *Más arriba de Cavendish Crescent se encuentra Somerset Place, de finales del siglo XVIII y diseñada por John Eveleigh.*

Camden Crescent was also designed by John Eveleigh. Its position on a steep hillside presented enormous technical challenges to combat landslips, and the grand design was never completed.

■*Camden Crescent a également été dessiné par John Eveleigh. Son emplacement sur une colline à pente raide constituait un défi technique énorme pour lutter contre les glissements de terrain, et ce grand projet n'a jamais été terminé.*

■*Camden Crescent, ebenfalls ein Entwurf von John Eveleigh. Die steile Hanglage stellte eine enorme technische Herausforderung dar, da die Gefahr von Erdrutschen unterbunden werden mußte, und der großartige Plan wurde nie zu Ende gebracht.*

■*Camden Crescent fue también diseñada por John Eveleigh. Al localizarse en una fuerte pendiente representó un desafío técnico muy grande ya que se enfrentaban con problemas de desprendimientos de tierra, el gran diseño nunca se completo.*

The Royal Crescent, described as the finest in Europe, consists of a sweeping arc of 30 houses standing behind a flourish of 114 columns. It was designed by John Wood the younger. The Duke of York lived in 1796 in Number 1, now a museum.

■*Le Royal Crescent, décrit comme le plus beau d'Europe, est un édifice élégant en arc de cercle composé de 30 maisons derrière 114 splendides colonnes. Il a été dessiné par John Wood fils. Le Duc de York vécut au Numéro 1 en 1796, devenu maintenant un musée.*

■*The Royal Crescent, das als das feinste Gebäude seiner Art in Europa beschrieben wurde, besteht aus dem geschwungenen Halbmond einer Häuserreihe von 30 Häusern hinter einem Bogen von 114 Säulen. Es wurde von John Wood dem Jüngeren entworfen. Im Haus Nr. 1 wohnte 1796 der Herzog von York, heute ist es ein Museum.*

■*El Royal Crescent, descrito como el más elegante de Europa, consiste en un majestuoso arco de 30 casas erguidas detrás de un despliegue de 114 columnas. Fue diseñado por John Wood el menor. En 1796 el Duke de York vivió en el Número 1, actualmente un museo.*

Marlborough Buildings, a long terrace, echoes the dignified development of the acclaimed Royal Crescent. It was built in the closing years of the 18th century.

■Marlborough Buildings, une longue rangée de maisons, évoque le développement du Royal Crescent tant acclamé. Sa construction eut lieu tout à la fin du 18ème siècle.

■In den Ende des 18. Jahrhunderts erbauten Marlborough Buildings, einer langen Häuserreihe, wiederholt sich die würdevolle Eleganz des berühmten Royal Crescent.

■Marlborough Buildings, un terraza amplia, resuena al majestuoso y aclamado conjunto de casas del Royal Crescent. Fue construido a finales del siglo XVIII.

BATH ABBEY

The west window points to the fan vaulted ceiling, the most spectacular architectural feature of the Abbey's interior.

■*Les fenêtres ouest sont tournées vers la voûte en éventail, l'une des caractéristiques les plus spectaculaires de l'intérieur de l'Abbaye.*

■*Das Westfenster weist zur Fächergewölbedecke, dem spektakulärsten architektonischen Merkmal im Inneren der Abbey.*

■*La ventana al Oeste apuntando hacia el raso de la bóveda en forma de abanico, es sin duda alguna el aspecto arquitectónico más destacado del interior de la Abadía.*

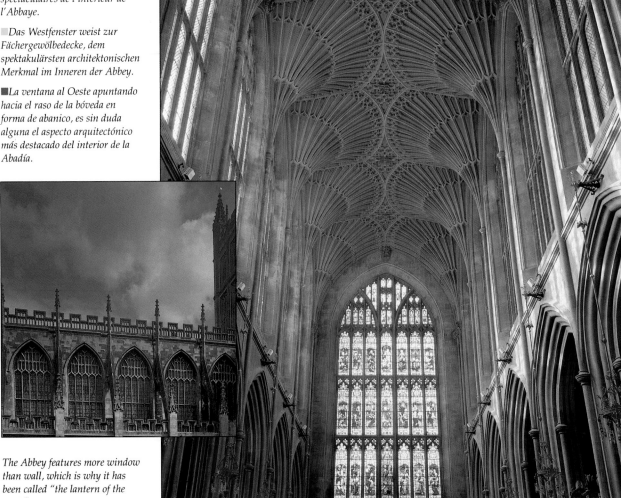

The Abbey features more window than wall, which is why it has been called "the lantern of the west."

■*L'abbaye comporte plus de fenêtres que de murs, et pour cette raison on l'appelle la "lanterne de l'ouest".*

■*Die Abbey hat mehr Fenster- als Wandfläche, daher ihre Bezeichnung als "Laterne des Westens".*

■*La Abadía al tener más ventanas que paredes, se la ha dado a conocer como "la linterna del Oeste".*

Bath Abbey and the Orange Grove, where an obelisk commemorates a visit of the Prince of Orange in 1734.

■*L'Abbaye de Bath et l'Orangeraie, où l'obélisque commémore une visite du Prince Guillaume d'Orange en 1734.*

■*Bath Abbey und Orange Grove, wo ein Obelisk an einen Besuch des Prinzen von Oranien im Jahr 1734 erinnert.*

■*La Abadía de Bath y Orange Grove, donde un obelísco conmemora la visita del Príncipe de Orange en 1734.*

The Abbey from the east, dramatically floodlit.

■*L'Abbaye vue de l'est, magnifiquement illuminée.*

■*Die Abbey von Osten mit dramatischer Flutlichtbeleuchtung.*

■*Vista desde el costado Este de la Abadía, dramáticamente iluminada.*

A detail of the nativity scene in the east window.

■*Détails de la crèche du vitrail est.*

■*Ein Ausschnitt aus dem Ostfenster, das die Geburt Christi darstellt.*

■*Un detalle de una escena navideña en la ventana Este.*

The carved oak West Door dates from the 17th century.

■*La porte ouest en chêne sculpté date du 17ème siècle.*

■*Das geschnitzte eicherne Westtor stammt aus dem 17. Jahrhundert.*

■*El roble carvado de la Puerta en el lado Oeste es de la época del siglo XVII.*

Bath Abbey organ, framed by the stone tracery of the fan vaulting.

■*L'orgue de l'Abbaye de Bath, encadré par le remplage en pierre de la voûte en éventail.*

■*Die Orgel der Bath Abbey, umrahmt vom Filigranmuster des Fächergewölbes.*

■*El órgano de la Abadía de Bath, encuadrado por la tracería en piedra de la bóveda en forma de abanico.*

Stone statues of St. Peter and St. Paul standing either side of the West Door.

■*Statues lapidaires de St. Pierre et St. Paul flanquant chaque côté de la porte occidentale.*

■*Steinstatuen von St. Petrus und St. Paulus neben der Westtür.*

■*Estatuas de piedra de San Pedro y San Pablo de pie a cada lado de la Puerta Occidental.*

Bishop Montague's tomb, the largest in the Abbey. He was responsible for an enthusiastic renovation programme in the 17th century.

■*La tombe de l'évêque Montague est la plus grande de l'Abbaye. Il fut à l'origine du programme de rénovation enthousiaste entrepris au 17ème siècle.*

■*Bischof Montagues Grabmahl, das größte in der Abbey. Er war im 17. Jahrhundert für ein enthusiastisches Restaurierungsprogramm verantwortlich.*

■*La tumba del Obispo Montague, la tumba más significativa de la Abadía. El Obispo Montague fue el responsable de iniciar un programa de renovación durante el siglo XVII.*

The Abbey's west front symbolically depicts the dream of Bishop Oliver King, of ladders reaching to heaven with falling and rising angels.

■*La façade ouest de l'Abbaye illustre de façon symbolique le rêve de l'évêque Oliver King, puisqu'elle est ornée d'échelles conduisant au paradis avec des anges montant et descendant.*

■*Die Westfront der Abbey stellt symbolisch den Traum von Bischof Oliver King dar: In den Himmel reichende Leitern und auf- und absteigenden Engel.*

■*La fachada al Oeste de la Abadía representa simbólicamente el sueño del Obispo Oliver King, de escaleras alcanzándo el cielo con ángeles ascendiendo y cayéndose.*

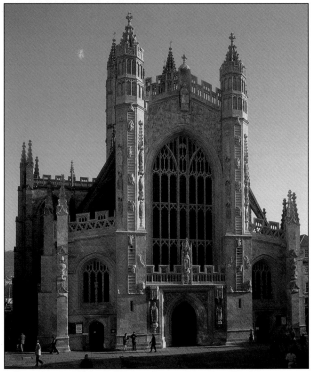

The present Abbey has stood dominant for five centuries at Bath's centre. Work on the present structure started in 1499.

■*L'Abbaye actuelle domine le centre de Bath depuis cinq siècles. Les travaux sur la structure actuelle ont commencé en 1499.*

■*Die derzeitige Abbey beherrscht schon seit fünf Jahrhunderten das Zentrum von Bath. Die Arbeiten am heutigen Gebäude begannen 1499.*

■*La Abadía actual se ha erguido prominentemente durante cinco siglo en el centro de Bath. Los trabajos del actual edificio comenzaron en 1499.*

BATH IN BLOOM

Tumbling from windows...

■*Tombant des fenêtres en cascades...*

■*Das blühende Bath zeigt sich in vielerlei Gestalt - an Fenstern ...*

■*Derramándose de las ventanas...*

Nodding under trees...

■*Se balançant sous les arbres...*

■*unter Bäumen ...*

■*Echándose una cabezada bajo los árboles...*

Prettying precincts...

■*Embellissant les centres commerciaux...*

■*und in Einkaufszentren ...*

■*Embelleziéndo recintos...*

Bursting from balconies...

■*Egayant les balcons...*

■*auf Balkonen ...*

■*Rebosando de los balcones..*

Fringing spires...

■*Effleurant les flèches..*

■*um Türme ...*

■*Orlando agujas...*

Topping walls...

■Parsemant les murs...

■auf Mauern ...

■Coronando piedras...

Enhancing parks...

■Accentuant la beauté des parcs...

■in Parks ...

■Realzando parques...

Framing windowsills...

■Encadrant les rebords de fenêtre...

■auf Fensterbänken ...

■Enmarcando antepechos...

Framing crescents...

■Bordant les rues en arc de cercle...

■an Fassaden ...

■Enmarcando calles en forma de arco...

Curtaining walls...

■*Couvrant les murs...*

■*an Wänden und Mauern.*

■*Cascándo de las paredes*

Encircling an obelisk...

■*Encerclant un obélisque...*

■*Obelisken umschlingend ...*

■*Envolviendo un obelisco...*

...wherever you look, Bath's blooms look blooming lovely!

■*... où que vous soyez à Bath, ses fleurs sont si jolies!*

■*Bath blüht und grünt an allen Ecken und Enden.*

■*... dondequiera que mire, Bath en flor es realmente bonita!*

BATH'S BRIDGES

Pulteney Bridge, built in 1770, was designed by Robert Adam, who won a competition for young architects. It is the only bridge in England with shops on both sides.

■Pulteney Bridge, construit en 1770, fut conçu par Robert Adam qui remporta un concours de jeunes architectes. C'est le seul pont en Angleterre avec des magasins des deux côtés.

■Pulteney Bridge wurde 1770 nach einem Entwurf von Robert Adam gebaut, der mit seinem Entwurf einen Wettbewerb für junge Architekten gewann. Pulteney Bridge ist die einzige Brücke in England mit Läden auf beiden Seiten.

■Pulteney Bridge, construido en 1770, fue diseñado por Robert Adam, quién ganó un concurso entre jóvenes arquitectos. Es el único puente en Inglaterra con tiendas en ambos lados.

After building his mansion – Prior Park – Ralph Allen, the owner of the stone quarry from which much of Georgian Bath was built, completed the view with a complementary Palladian-style Bridge, built in 1755.

■Après avoir fait construire son château - Prior Park - Ralph Allen, le propriétaire des carrières qui ont donné la plus grande partie de la ville de Bath au 18ème siècle, y fit ajouter un pont style palladien, construit en 1755.

■Nach dem Bau seines Herrenhauses Prior Park vervollständigte Ralph Allen seine Aussicht 1755 mit einer ergänzenden Brücke im palladianischen Stil. Ralph Allen war der Eigentümer des Steinbruchs, aus dem das Material für die meisten der Bauten im georgianischen Bath kam.

■Después de haber construido su mansión - Prior Park - Ralph Allen, el propietario de la cantera de donde procedía casi toda la piedra con la que se construyó la ciudad de Bath durante la época Georgiana, completo la panorámica de su casa con un Puente de estilo Paladesco, construído en 1755.

The present North Parade Bridge dates from 1945.

■ *Le pont actuel North Parade Bridge date de 1945.*

■ *Die heutige North Parade Bridge wurde 1945 gebaut.*

■ *El actual North Parade Bridge data de 1945.*

Cleveland House, bridging the Kennet and Avon Canal.

■ *Cleveland House, construite au-dessus du Kennet & Avon Canal.*

■ *Cleveland House überbrückt den Kennet-Avon-Kanal.*

■ *Cleveland House, tendiéndo un puente entre Kennet y Avon Canal.*

Shops on Pulteney Bridge.

■Des magasins sur Pulteney Bridge.

▢Läden auf der Pulteney Bridge.

■Tiendas en Pulteney Bridge.

As dusk falls, floodlights enhance the arched elegance of Pulteney Bridge.

■Au crépuscule, des projecteurs accentuent davantage l'élégance des trois arches de Pulteney Bridge.

▢In der Abenddämmerung werden die eleganten Bögen der Pulteney Bridge durch Flutlicht verzaubert.

■Al caer el crepúsculo, las iluminaciónes embellecen la elegancia del arcado de Pulteney Bridge.

BATH'S BUILDINGS

Stone sentinels at Number 8 Bath Street. Bath Street with its twin rows of columns was designed to give covered access between King's Bath and Cross and Hot Baths.

■Sentinelles en pierre au Numéro 8 de Bath Street. Bath Street avec ses doubles rangées de colonnes a été conçue pour offrir un passage couvert entre King's Bath, Cross Bath et Hot Baths.

■Steinwächter vor 8 Bath Street. Bath Street mit seiner doppelten Säulenallee wurde als überdachter Zugang zwischen Königsbad (King's Bath) und Kreuz- (Cross Bath) und Heißem Bad (Hot Bath) gebaut.

■Centinelas de piedra en el Número 8 de Bath Street. Bath Street con su fila doble de columnas fue diseñado para dar una entrada cubierta entre King's Bath y Cross y Hot Baths.

Prior Park College is the grandest Palladian-style mansion in Britain. It was built for Ralph Allen, the entrepreneur whose quarries provided the stone for the building of 18th century Bath.

■Prior Park College est le plus beau château style palladien en Grande-Bretagne. Il a été construit pour Ralph Allen, l'entrepreneur dont les carrières fournirent les pierres pour la construction de Bath au 18ème siècle.

■Prior Park College ist das prachtvollste Herrenhaus im palladianischen Stil in Großbritannien. Es wurde für Ralph Allen erbaut, den Unternehmer, dessen Steinbrüche das Material für den Bau des georgianischen Bath (18. Jahrhundert) lieferten.

■Prior Park College es la mansión más resplendorosa de estilo Paladesco en Gran Bretaña. Fue construida por Ralph Allen, un hombre de negocios cuyas canteras proporcionaron la piedra para la construcción del Bath del siglo XVIII.

Above the medieval City Wall stands the Royal Mineral Water Hospital, dating from 1737. Thousands visited hoping the waters would bring miraculous cures for conditions as varied as palsies and piles.

■Au-dessus du Mur médiéval de la ville, se dresse le Royal Mineral Water Hospital datant de 1737. Des milliers de personnes se sont rendues aux sources en espérant qu'elles pourraient guérir miraculeusement des maladies variées telles que paralysies et hémorroïdes.

■Über der mittelalterlichen Stadtmauer steht das Royal Mineral Water Hospital aus dem Jahr 1737. Es wurde von vielen Tausenden besucht, die sich von dem Mineralwasser wunderbare Heilung für die verschiedensten Krankheiten erhofften.

■Por encima del medieval City Wall se encuentra el Royal Mineral Water Hospital, el cual data de 1737. Miles de personas visitaron éste Hospital en la espera de encontrar en sus aguas curas milagrosas para condiciones tan diversas como parálisis y hemorroides.

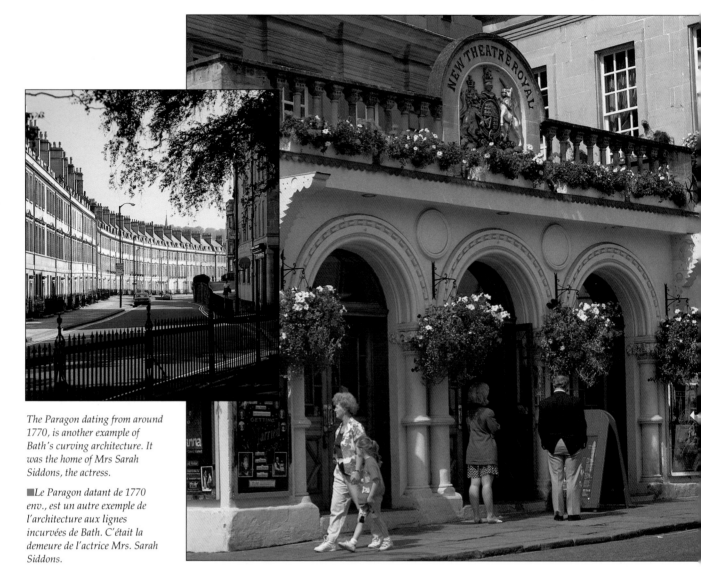

The Paragon dating from around 1770, is another example of Bath's curving architecture. It was the home of Mrs Sarah Siddons, the actress.

■Le Paragon datant de 1770 env., est un autre exemple de l'architecture aux lignes incurvées de Bath. C'était la demeure de l'actrice Mrs. Sarah Siddons.

■Das Paragon, etwa aus dem Jahr 1770, ist ein weiteres Beispiel für die geschwungenen, bogenreichen Bauten von Bath. Hier wohnte die Schauspielerin Sarah Siddons.

■El Paragon data aproximadamente de 1770, y es otro ejemplar de la arquitectura curvada de Bath. Fue el hogar de la actriz Sarah Siddons.

The Circus – John Wood's greatest work. The frieze shows symbols of the arts and sciences. It attracted famous and distinguished residents – including Lord Clive of India and Horace Walpole.

■Le Circus - la plus belle création de John Wood. La frise représente des symbole des arts et de la science. Il a attiré des résidents célèbres et éminents - dont Lord Clive d'Inde et Horace Walpole.

■The Circus - John Woods größtes Werk. Das Fries enthält Symbole der Künste und Wissenschaften. Hier wohnten berühmte und distinguierte Persönlichkeiten, darunter Lord Clive von Indien und Horace Walpole.

■El Circus - obra maestra de John Wood. El friso muestra símbolos de las artes y las ciencias... Este barrio atrajo residentes famosos y distinguidos - entre ellos Lord Clive de las Indias y Horacio Walpole.

The Theatre Royal, built in 1805, though the interior was gutted by fire half a century later. Next to it is Beau Nash's first house in Bath.

■Le Théâtre Royal, construit en 1805; malheureusement l'intérieur fut détruit par un incendie un siècle plus tard. La première maison de Beau Nash à Bath est adjacente.

■Das Theatre Royal wurde 1805 erbaut, brannte jedoch ein halbes Jahrhundert später aus. Daneben befindet sich Beau Nashs erstes Haus in Bath.

■El Teatro Real, construido en 1805, desafortunadamente su interior fue destruido en un fuego medio siglo más tarde. A su lado se encuentra la primera casa de Beau Nash en Bath.

Gentle, graceful curves in The Royal Crescent.

■Les courbes douces et élégantes du Royal Crescent.

■Sanfte, elegant geschwungene Bögen im Royal Crescent.

■Curvas suaves y elegantes del Royal Crescent.

The Cross Bath, rebuilt at the end of the 18th century, is fed by one of the city's three hot springs.

■Le Cross Bath, reconstruit à la fin du 18ème siècle, est alimenté par l'une des trois sources thermales de la ville.

■Das gegen Ende des 18.

Jahrhunderts wieder aufgebaute Kreuzbad (Cross Bath) wird von einer der drei heißen Quellen der Stadt gespeist.

■Cross Bath, reconstruido a finales del siglo XVIII, se alimenta en uno de los tres mantiales de agua caliente de la ciudad.

As well as a 'country' mansion, the entrepreneur Ralph Allen had a 'town' house tucked off York Street. It was designed by John Wood the Elder.

■*En plus de son château "à la campagne", l'entrepreneur Ralph Allen avait également une maison "en ville" nichée dans York Street. Elle a été dessinée par John Wood père.*

■*Neben seinem Landhaus hatte der Unternehmer Ralph Allen in der Nähe der York Street auch ein von John Wood dem Älteren entworfenes Stadthaus.*

■*Al igual que una casa de "campo", Ralph Allen, hombre de negocios tenía una casa en la "ciudad" recojida en York Street. Fue diseñada por John Wood el Mayor.*

In Abbey Churchyard can be found Field Marshall Wade's house, dating from 1720. Above the shopfront are fine carved garlands between carved Corinthian pilasters.

■*Dans l'Abbey Churchyard on peut trouver la maison du Field Marshall Wade, qui date de 1720. Au-dessus de la devanture du magasin on peut voir de belles guirlandes entre des pilastres corinthiens sculptés.*

■*Auf dem Abbey Churchyard befindet sich das Haus von Feldmarschall Wade, das 1720 erbaut wurde. über der Ladenfront ist es mit kunstvoll gemeißelten Girlanden zwischen korinthischen Pilastern verziert.*

■*En el Cementerio de la Abadía se puede encontrar la casa del Mariscal de Campo Wade, data de 1720. Encima del escaparate se puede ver las elegantes guirnaldas esculpidas entre los pilastros carvados de estilo Coríntio.*

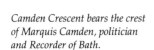

Camden Crescent bears the crest of Marquis Camden, politician and Recorder of Bath.

■*Camden Crescent arbore les armoiries du Marquis Camden, politicien et Avocat de Bath nommé par la Couronne.*

■*Camden Crescent trägt das Wappen des Marquis Camden, einem Politiker und Chronisten von Bath.*

■*Camden Crescent lleva la cresta del Marqués Camden, político y Registrador de Bath.*

BATH BUNS, BALLS AND BANQUETS

The Pump Room where Beau Nash's statue proclaims his reign as society king of Georgian Bath. He laid down the rules for banquets, breakfasts, dances and musical entertainments.

■La Salle des pompes et la statue de Beau Nash proclamant son règne en tant que roi de la haute société de Bath au 18ème siècle. Il établit l'étiquette pour les banquets, les petits déjeuners, la danse et les divertissements musicaux.

■Die Trinkhalle, in der die Statue von Beau Nash seine Herrschaft als Gesellschaftskönig des georgianischen Bath erklärt. Beau Nash setzte die gesellschaftlichen Regeln für Bankette, Frühstücke, Tänze und musikalische Unterhaltung fest.

■La Sala de Bombeo donde la estatua de Beau Nash proclama su reino como rey de la sociedad de Bath durante la época Georgiana. Beau Nath estableció las reglas para los banquetes, desayunos, bailes y entretenimientos musicales.

To this elegant Corinthian-columned Pump Room, fashionable society made their regular visits to drink the water – three glasses in the morning were recommended by Georgian physicians.

■Le beau monde se rendait régulièrement dans cette élégante Salle des pompes aux colonnes corinthiennes, pour y boire l'eau - les médecins de l'époque recommandaient trois verres le matin.

■Die Vornehmen der Gesellschaft besuchten diese elegante Trinhalle mit ihren korinthischen Säulen regelmäßig für ihre Trinkkuren - georgianische Ärzte empfahlen morgens drei Gläser des Mineralwassers.

■Gente de sociedad de moda venían frequentemente a ésta elegante Sala de Bombeo con columnas Coríntias para beber sus aguas - los médicos de la época Georgiana recomendaban beber tres vasos por la mañanas.

The toast of Bath – water – tastes as if it ought to be medicinal: a cocktail containing 40 different minerals and elements, flowing from the King's Spring in the Pump Room.

■L'attraction de Bath - son eau - a le goût d'un produit médicinal: un mélange contenant 40 composants et minéraux différents, s'écoulant de la Source du roi (King's Spring) dans la Salle des pompes.

■Der gefeierte Mittelpunkt von Bath - sein Wasser - schmeckt schon wie eine Medizin. Es enthält 40 verschiedene Mineralien und Elemente und fließt aus der Königsquelle (King's Spring) in die Trinkhalle (Pump Room).

■El brindis de Bath - agua - sabe como si debiera ser una poción medicinal: un cocktail de 40 minerales y elementos distintos, manando del King's Spring en la Sala de Bombeo.

The Guildhall, dating from 1776
was designed by Thomas
Baldwin as a venue for balls for
wealthy traders of Bath.

■L'Hôtel de ville, qui date de
1766, a été dessiné par Thomas
Baldwin en tant que lieu de bals
pour les négociants fortunés de
Bath.

■Die Guildhall aus dem Jahr
1766 wurde von Thomas
Baldwin als Veranstaltungsort
für die Bälle der reichen Händler
von Bath entworfen.

■El Ayuntamiento, data de
1766, fue diseñado por Thomas
Baldwin como lugar de reunión
donde los ricos comerciantes de
Bath daban fiestas.

Twentieth century refreshment.

■*Des rafraîchissements du vingtième siècle.*

■*Erfrischungen im Stil des zwanzigsten Jahrhunderts.*

■*Refrescos del siglo XX.*

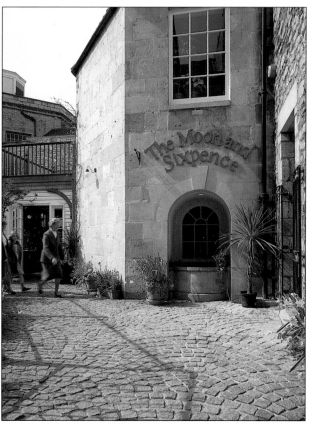

Cobbled courtyard entrance to the Moon and Sixpence restaurant.

■*L'entrée pavée de la cour du restaurant "Moon and Sixpence".*

■*Gepflasterte Hofeinfahrt zum Restaurant Moon and Sixpence.*

■*Entrada al patio adoquinado del restaurante Moon and Sixpence.*

The Guildhall contains the Banqueting Hall, one of the finest rooms in the Adam style in Europe.

■*L'Hôtel de ville renferme le Hall des banquets, l'une des plus belles pièces style Adam, en Europe.*

■*Die Guildhall enthält die Banqueting Hall, einen der feinsten Säle im Adam-Stil in Europa.*

■*En el Ayuntamiento se puede encontrar la Sala de Banquetes, una de las salas más elegantes en Europa de estilo Adam.*

The three bars below the wine bar lead to a short cut from the Paragon to Walcot Street.

■*Les trois bars après le wine bar conduisent à un raccourci pour aller du Paragon à Walcot Street.*

■*Die drei schmiedeeisernen Pfosten unterhalb des Weinlokals führen zu einer Abkürzung vom Paragon zur Walcot Street.*

■*Las tres barras debajo de la tasca de vinos llevan a un atajo entre Paragon y Walcot Street.*

Sally Lunn's house in North Parade Passage is the oldest house in Bath, now a refreshment house. Sally Lunn arrived in the city in 1680 to bake and hawk her brioche buns, still cooked to her secret recipe today.

■La maison de Sally Lunn dans le North Parade Passage est la plus vieille maison de Bath, transformée aujourd'hui en salon de thé. Sally Lunn arriva dans la ville en 1680 pour colporter ses brioches, que l'on prépare encore aujourd'hui en suivant sa recette secrète

■Sally Lunns Haus in der North Parade Passage ist das älteste Haus in Bath, heute enthält es eine Teestube. Sally Lunn kam 1680 nach Bath, um ihr Brioche-Gebäck, die sogenannten Bath Buns, zu backen und feilzuhalten. Diese Buns werden immer noch nach ihrem geheimen Rezept hergestellt.

■La casa de Sally Lunn en North Parade Passage es la casa más antigua de Bath, actualmente una casa de refrescos. Sally Lunn llegó a la ciudad de Bath en 1680 con la intención de hornear y vender por las calles sus bollos, hoy en día se sigue haciendo éstos bollos de acuerdo con su receta secreta.

Teatime in Shire's Yard, celebration of a centuries-old ritual.

■L'heure du thé à Shire's Yard, la célébration d'une tradition remontant à plusieurs siècles.

■Teatime in Shire's Yard - ein jahrhundertealter Brauch.

■La Hora del Té en Shire's Yard, celebración de un ritual de más de un siglo.

BOULEVARDS, BOUTIQUES AND BUSKERS

Buskers entertain the tourists outside the Pump Room.

■*Les baladins distraient les touristes en face de la Salle des pompes (Pump Room).*

■*Straßenmusikanten vor der Trinkhalle (Pump Room) unterhalten die Touristen.*

■*Fuera de la Sala de Bombeo, músicos ambulantes entretienen los turístas.*

Trim Street's development began in 1707 – part of the first significant building boom of the 18th century. Trymme Street owed its name to George Trymme, a gentleman clothier.

■*Trim Street a commencé à être développée en 1707, lors de l'essor des constructions au 18ème siècle. Trymme Street doit son nom à George Trymme, drapier éminent.*

■*Mit dem Bau der Trim Street wurde 1707 begonnen. Das Projekt war Teil des ersten bedeutenden Baubooms des 18. Jahrhunderts. Trymme Street wurde nach George Trymme benannt, einem Herrenausstatter.*

■*El desarrollo de Trim Street empezó en 1707 - fue la primera faceta de un importante boom en construcción durante el siglo XVIII. Trim Street debe su nombre a George Trymme, un caballero sastre.*

Pipe music, appropriately played outside the Pump Room in Abbey Churchyard.

■*Un musicien joue de la flûte, instrument approprié, en face de la Salle des pompes dans l'Abbey Churchyard.*

■*Flötenmusik vor der Trinhalle auf dem Abbey Churchyard.*

■*Fuera de la Sala de Bombeo en el Cementerio de la Abadía se toca, como debe ser, música de gaita.*

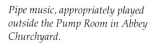

Laura Place with its stone fountain is the prelude to Bath's most impressive boulevard, Great Pulteney Street.

■Laura Place, avec sa fontaine en pierre, est le prélude du boulevard le plus impressionnant de Bath, Great Pulteney Street.

■Laura Place mit seinem Steinbrunnen bildet den Auftakt zum eindrucksvollsten Boulevard in Bath: Great Pulteney Street.

■Laura Place con su fuente de piedra es el preludio al bulevar más impresionante de Bath, Great Pulteney Street.

The boutiques and browsers in New Bond Street Place.

■Les boutiques et les flâneurs sur la Place New Bond Street.

□Die Boutiken und Einkäufer in New Bond Street Place.

■Las boutiques y gente paseando por New Bond Street Place.

Abbey Green is the site of the monastic buildings of an early priory – an iron hook from its gatehouse is all that remains.

■Abbey Green est le site de bâtiments monacaux d'un ancien prieuré - un crochet en fer de la loge de garde en est le seul vestige.

■Abbey Green ist die Stätte der Klostergebäude eines frühen Priorats. Übrig ist heute nur noch ein eiserner Haken von seinem Pförtnerhaus.

■Abbey Green es donde se erguían los edificios monásticos de un anterior priorato - un gancho de hierro perteneciente a la antigua puerta de entrada es todo lo que queda del edificio.

46

North Parade Passage bathed in sunshine with a glimpse of Sham Castle.

■Passage de North Parade inondé des rayons du soleil avec aperçu sur Sham Castle.

■Die sonnenüberflutete North Parade Passage mit Blick auf Sham Castle..

■El Pasaje de North Parade bañado por el sol, donde se vislumbra el Sham Castle.

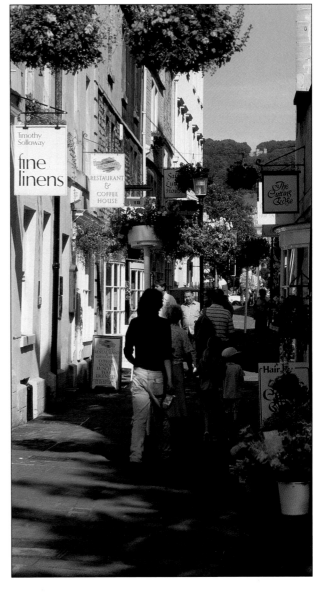

Northumberland Place, a haven for strollers and shoppers.

■Northumberland Place, véritable paradis pour les promenades et les achats.

■Northumberland Place, ein Paradies für Schaufensterbummel, Einkäufe und Spaziergänge.

■Northumberland Place, un refugio para paseantes y gentes de compras.

47

BOTANICAL BATH

Plants from all over the world provide a constantly changing kaleidoscope of colour in the ...ical Gardens. In spring ...

■Des plantes des quatre coins du monde offrent un kaléïdoscope aux couleurs changeantes dans les Jardins Botaniques. Au printemps...

■Im Botanischen Garten sorgen Pflanzen aus allen Teilen der Welt für ein sich ständig änderndes Farbenkaleidoskop: Im Frühling ...

■Plantas traídas de todo el mundo proporcionan un calidoscopio de cambios de colores contínuos en los Jardines Botánicos. En Primavera...

...in summer...

■En été...

■... im Sommer ...

■En verano...

... and in winter.

■...et en hiver.

■... und im Winter.

■... y en invierno.

The Temple of Minerva in Sydney Gardens, the oldest park in Bath. It was famous as a rendezvous in the 18th and 19th centuries.

■Le Temple de Minerva dans les jardins de Sydney, le plus vieux parc de Bath. C'était un lieu de rendez-vous célèbre aux 18ème et 19ème siècles.

■Der Tempel der Minerva in Sydney Gardens, dem ältesten Park in Bath. Der Park war im 18. und 19. Jahrhundert ein berühmter Treffpunkt.

■El Templo de Minerva en Sydney Gardens, el parque más antiguo en Bath. Un lugar de rendezvous muy famoso durante los siglos XVIII y XIX.

The different shades of green indicate some of the 5,000 different species of plants and trees to be found in the Botanical Gardens.

■Les différentes nuances de vert indiquent les 5.000 espèces différentes de plantes et d'arbres que l'on peut trouver dans les Jardins Botaniques.

■Die unterschiedlichen Grüntöne lassen auf einige der 5.000 verschiedenen Pflanzenarten im Botanischen Garten schließen.

■Los distintos matices de verde muestran algunas de las diversas 5,000 especies de plantas y árboles que se pueden encontrar en los Jardines Botánicos.

The sound of water and the scent of plants (complete with Braille labels) provide a garden for the blind in Henrietta Park.

■Le bruit de l'eau et la senteur des plantes (avec des étiquettes en braille) offrent un jardin agréable pour les aveugles dans Henrietta Park.

■Im Henrietta Park entstand ein Park für Blinde und Sehbehinderte, die seine Schönheit über die Geräusche des Wassers und den Duft der Pflanzen (komplett mit Blindenschrift-Schildern) genießen können.

■El sonidos de las aguas y el aroma de las plantas (con etiquetas en Braille y todo) - el Jardín Henrietta Park proporciona un jardín para los ciegos.

Bath and Business

Tourism is the main business of Bath. Shoppers and strollers in Union Street.

■Le tourisme est la principale activité commerciale de Bath. Union Street: rue où l'on fait ses emplettes et où l'on flâne.

■Tourismus ist der bedeutendste Wirtschaftszweig für Bath. Einkäufer und Spaziergänger in Union Street.

■Turismo es la industria más importante de Bath. Gente de compras y paseantes en Union Street.

Business is breathing new life into converted warehouses on the riverbank.

■Le milieu des affaires redonne un souffle de vie aux entrepôts reconvertis sur la rive.

■Umgebaute Lagerhäuser am Flußufer haben neue Aufgaben und neues Leben erhalten.

■El establecimiento de nuevos negocios en almacenes reconvertidos en las orillas del río alientan prosperidad a la zona.

Upwardly mobile at the Podium shopping mall.

■Elégant Escalier roulant ultra-moderne dans la galerie marchande Podium.

■Im Podium-Einkaufszentrum.

■Gente bien en el centro comercial Podium.

The Podium is a 20th century 'cathedral to commerce' in neo classic style.

■Le Podium est une "cathédrale du commerce" du 20ème siècle de style néo-classique.

■Das im klassizistischen Stil erbaute Podium ist eine "Kommerzkathedrale" des 20. Jahrhunderts.

■El Podium construido en un estilo neo-clásico es la "catedral del comercio" del siglo XX .

Milsom Street, named after a canny 18th century wine cooper and property speculator. Designed by John Wood the Elder, building started in 1762.

■Milsom Street porte le nom d'un fabricant de tonneaux et spéculateur immobilier malin du 18ème siècle. Elle fut dessinée par John Wood père et la construction commença en 1762.

■Milsom Street wurde nach einem sparsamen Küfer und Immobilienspekulanten des 18. Jahrhunderts benannt. Milsom Street wurde von John Wood dem Älteren entworfen, mit ihrem Bau wurde 1762 begonnen.

■Milsom Street, debe su nombre a un astuto tonelero de vinos y especulador en terrenos del siglo XVIII. Diseñado por John Wood el Mayor, los trabajos de construcción comenzaron en 1762.

The 19th century covered market in the High Street contains a market pillar or 'nail'. Upon it, deals were struck. The term 'to pay on the nail' refers to cash transactions conducted in this way.

■Le marché couvert du 19ème siècle dans la High Street (grand-rue) comporte un pilier de marché ou "nail" (signifiant également "ongle"). On y concluait des marchés et l'expression "to pay on the nail" (payer rubis sur l'ongle) réfère aux transactions en argent comptant faites de cette façon.

■Der überdachte Markt aus dem 19. Jahrhundert in der High Street enthält eine Marktsäule, "Nail" genannt, die zum Abschließen von Geschäften und als Zahlungspunkt diente.

■El mercado al cubierto del siglo XIX en la High Street tiene un mercado con columnas o "clavo". Entre sus paredes, se acordaron negocios. La expresión "pagar en el clavo" se refiere a transacciones en efectivo llevadas a cabo de ésta manera.

BATH BEDECKED

Pulteney Bridge and weir in
winter.

■Le pont Pulteney et le barrage
en hiver.

▢Pulteney Bridge und Wehr im
Winter.

■Pulteney Bridge y cañal en
invierno.

A study in snow and stone –
Lansdown and Cavendish
Crescents.

■Une étude neige et pierre -
Lansdown Crescent et Cavendish
Crescent.

▢Eine Studie aus Schnee und
Stein - Lansdown Cresent und
Cavendish Crescent.

■Un estudio en nieve y piedra -
Lansdown y Cavendish
Crescents.

The broad, fashionable pavements of Milsom Street joined together with Christmas lights.

■Les trottoirs larges de la rue très courue Milsom Street, décorée par les illuminations de Noël.

■Weihnachtsbeleuchtung verbindet die breiten, modernen Gehsteige der Milsom Street.

■Las amplias y elegantes aceras de Milsom Street galardonadas con luces de Navidad.

Christmas is announced in Abbey Green.

■Noël est annoncé à l'Abbey Green.

■Die Weihnachtszeit beginnt in Abbey Green.

■Proclamación de la Navidad en Abbey Green.

Cavendish Place.

■Cavendish Place.

■Cavendish Place.

■Cavendish Place.

THE BEST OF BATH

Prior Park, former home of one of Bath's most famous Georgian residents. Ralph Allen, born 1693, bought the quarries on Combe Down and built his mansion to show the superb qualities of the stone.

■*Prior park, ancienne demeure de l'un des plus célèbres résidents de Bath au 18ème siècle. Ralph Allen, né en 1693 acheta les carrières de Combe Down et fit construire son château pour montrer les qualités superbes de la pierre.*

■*Prior Park, ehemals Wohnsitz eines der berühmtesten Bürger im georgianischen Bath. Ralph Allen, geboren 1693, kaufte die Steinbrüche an Combe Down und baute sein Herrenhaus, um die hervorragenden Eigenschaften des Steins zur Schau zu stellen.*

■*Prior Park, anteriormente el hogar de uno de los residentes más famosos de Bath durante la época Georgiana. Ralph Allen, nacido en 1693, adquirió la cantera de Combe Down y construyó su mansión como muestra ejemplar de las calidades únicas de la piedra que se extraía en su cantera.*

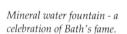

Bath's medieval East Gate.

■*La Porte Est médiévale de Bath.*

■*Das mittelalterliche Osttor (East Gate).*

■*East Gate - puerta de la época medieval en Bath.*

Mineral water fountain - a celebration of Bath's fame.

■*Fontaine d'eau minérale - une célébration de ce qui fit la réputation de Bath.*

■*Der Mineralwasser-Springbrunnen - der Berühmtheit der Stadt gewidmet.*

■*La fuente de agua mineral - una celebración de la fama de Bath.*

The Abbey and the Avon.

■ L'Abbaye et l'Avon.

□ Die Abbey und der Avon.

■ La Abadía y el Avon.

Somerset Place, designed in 1793 by the architect John Eveleigh. He was declared bankrupt the same year and never practised in Bath again.

■ Somerset Place, dessinée en 1793 par l'architecte John Eveleigh. Il fit faillite la même année et ne travailla plus jamais à Bath.

■ Somerset Place wurde 1793 vom Architekten John Eveleigh entworfen. Er wurde noch im gleichen Jahr bankrott erklärt und war nie wieder in Bath tätig.

■ Somerset Place, diseñada en 1793 por el arquitecto John Eveleigh. Este arquitecto fue declarado en quiebra ése mismo año y no ejerció nunca más su profesión en Bath.

An idea by Mr John Palmer, a wealthy brewer and chandler, led to the building of a theatre in Orchard Street in 1747. By 1767 it was granted the status of a Theatre Royal. The former elegant entrance stars in this picture.

■*Une idée de John Palmer, brasseur et épicier-droguiste, entraîna la construction d'un théâtre dans Orchard Street en 1747. Dès 1767, il obtint la statut de Théâtre Royal. Cette illustration montre l'ancienne entrée élégante du théatre.*

■*Eine Idee von John Palmer, einem reichen Bierbrauer, führte 1747 zum Bau eines Theaters in Orchard Street. 1767 wurde es zum Theatre Royal erklärt. Besonders eindrucksvoll ist der ehemalige elegante Eingang.*

■*Una idea que tuvo el Sr John Palmer, cervecero y velero pudiente, resultó en la construcción de un teatro en Orchard Street en 1747. En 1767 éste teatro fue otorgado la categoría de Teatro Real. En ésta fotografía figura la antigua elegante entrada.*

The Royal Crescent - an architectural masterpiece.

■*Le Royal Crescent - un chef-d'oeuvre architectural.*

■*Royal Crescent - ein architektonisches Meisterwerk.*

■*El Royal Crescent - una obra maestra en arquitectura.*

Blue skies, and the sound of leather on willow: Bath's annual cricket festival.

■*Un ciel bleu et le bruit du cuir sur le saule: le festival annuel de cricket de Bath.*

■*Blauer Himmel und ein typisch englischer Sport: Das jährliche Cricket-Fest von Bath.*

■*Cielos despejados, el sonido de cuero golpeando madera de sauce: el festival anual de Cricket en Bath.*

Lansdown Crescent, once the town address of the writer and eccentric millionaire, William Beckford.

■*Lansdown Crescent, ancienne adresse en ville de l'écrivain et millionnaire excentrique, William Beckford.*

■*Zu den Bewohnern von Lansdown Crescent gehörte auch der Schriftsteller und exzentrische Millionär William Beckford.*

■*Lansdown Crescent, fue una vez las señas usadas por el excéntrico millonario escritor, William Beckford cuando residió en la ciudad.*

The foundation stone for the new Guildhall was laid in 1768, to the accompaniment of a guinea's worth of Abbey bellringing. Designed by Thomas Baldwin, it has a sumptuous Banqueting Hall inside.

■*La première pierre du nouvel Hôtel de ville fut posée en 1768, cérémonie accompagnée d'une volée de cloches à l'Abbaye pour une guinée. Conçu par Thomas Baldwin, il renferme une salle de banquets somptueuse .*

■*Der Grundstein für die neue Guildhall wurde 1768 zum Klang der zu diesem Anlaß geläuteten Abbey-Glocken gelegt. Im Inneren des von Thomas Baldwin entworfenen Gebäudes befindet sich ein aufwendiger Festsaal.*

■*La primera piedra del nuevo edificio del Ayuntamiento fue colocada en 1768, éste acontecimiento fue acompañado con toques de campana en la Abadía por un valor de una guinea. Diseñada por Thomas Baldwin, en su interior hay una sumptuosa sala de Banquetes.*

Sham Castle was built by Ralph Allen to enhance the view from his town house in Bath. It dates from 1762.

■*Sham Castle a été construit par Ralph Allen pour avoir une plus belle vue de sa maison en ville. Ce château date de 1762.*

■*Sham Castle wurde 1762 von Ralph Allen gebaut, um ihm die Aussicht von seinem Stadthaus in Bath zu verschönern.*

■*Sham Castle fue construido por Ralph Allen para embellecer la vista desde su casa en la ciudad de Bath. Data de 1762.*

BACKDROP TO BATH

From Perfect View, Bath lies in a fold between the hills. Prior Park College commands another perfect view in the distance.

■Une vue parfaite: Bath nichée dans un creux entre les collines. Prior Park College offre une autre vue splendide au lointain.

■Aussicht von Perfect View: Bath liegt in einer Falte zwischen den Hügeln.

■Desde Perfect View, Bath yace en un pliegue entre las colinas. Prior Park College presenta otra panorámica perfecta en la distancia.

View towards Bath from Sally-in-the-Woods to the west.

■Vue sur Bath depuis Sally-in-the-Woods vers l'ouest.

■Blick in Richtung Bath von Sally-in-the-Woods, das westlich von der Stadt liegt.

■Panorámica de Bath desde Sally-in-the-Wood al Oeste.

To the north of the city lies the graceful Lansdown Crescent snaking its way across the hillside.

■*Situé au nord de la ville, l'élégant Lansdown Crescent serpente au flanc de la colline.*

■*Im Norden der Stadt liegt der charmante Lansdown Crescent, der mit vielen Windungen über den Abhang führt.*

■*Al norte de la ciudad se encuentra el elegante Landsdown Crescent que serpentea a través del flanco de la colina.*

Balloons setting off from Victoria Park on a still, clear evening.

■*Des ballons s'élèvent dans le ciel au-dessus de Victoria Park par une belle soirée.*

■*Heißluftballons beim Start in Victoria Park an einem ruhigen, klaren Abend.*

■*Globos despegándo en Victoria Park en una tarde apacible y despejada.*

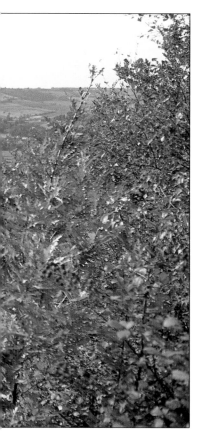

Cityscape from Beechen Cliff.

■Paysage urbain de Beechen Cliff.

■Blick auf die Stadt von Beechen Cliff.

■Paisaje urbano desde Beechen Cliff.

Sandwiched between snow - view of the city with Royal Crescent, the Abbey and Pulteney Bridge.

■Vue de la ville parsemée de neige montrant le Royal Crescent, l'Abbaye et le pont Pulteney Bridge.

■Blick auf die schneebedeckte Stadt mit Royal Crescent, Abbey und Pulteney Bridge.

■Apretujada entre la nieve - panorámica de la ciudad con el Royal Crescent, la Abadía y Pulteney Bridge.

BATH'S BACKWATERS AND BY-WAYS AND BEYOND

View of Bath from the Kennet and Avon Canal. It was opened in 1810.

■Vue de Bath depuis le Kennet & Avon Canal, ouvert en 1810.

■Blick auf Bath vom Kennet-Avon-Kanal, der 1810 eröffnet wurde.

■Vista de Bath desde el Kennet y Avon Canal. Fue inaugurado en 1810.

On Lansdown Hill lies the tomb of Bath's eccentric millionaire - the writer and misanthrope, William Beckford.

■Sur la colline Lansdown Hill se trouve la tombe du millionnaire excentrique de Bath - l'écrivain et misanthrope, William Beckford.

■Auf Lansdown Hill befindet sich das Grab des exzentrischen Millionärs von Bath - dem Schriftsteller und Misanthrop William Beckford.

■En la colina Lansdown yace la tumba del excéntrico millonario de Bath - el escritor y misántropo, William Beckford.

The weir at nearby Bathampton.

■Barrage à Bathampton, à proximité.

■Das Wehr bei Bathampton.

■El cañal cerca de Bathampton.

Claverton Manor has two flags flying: the Stars and Stripes and the Union Jack. This classical building in the English countryside is home to a museum of American domestic life from the late 17th to the middle of the 19th century.

■Claverton Manor arbore deux drapeaux: Le drapeau américain et le drapeau anglais. Ce bâtiment classique de la campagne anglaise abrite un musée de la vie domestique américaine de la fin du 17ème siècle au milieu du 19ème siècle.

■Auf Claverton Manor fliegen zwei Flaggen: Die "Stars and Stripes" der USA und der britische "Union Jack". In diesem klassischen Gebäude befindet sich ein Museum über Wohnen und Alltag im Amerika der Zeit vom 17. Jahrhundert bis zur Mitte des 19. Jahrhunderts.

■Claverton Manor tiene dos banderas izadas - la bandera estrellada y la bandera del Reino Unido. Este edificio clásico en la campiña inglesa, es hogar a un museo que recoge la vida doméstica Americana de finales del siglo XVII hasta mediados del siglo XIX.

Beckford's Tower, built in 1827 for William Beckford, has 156 steps up to a small museum dedicated to him.

■La Tour de Beckford, construite en 1827 pour William Beckford, comporte 156 marches conduisant à un petit musée qui lui a été dédié.

■Beckford's Tower wurde 1827 für William Beckford gebaut. Im Turm führen 156 Stufen zu einem kleinen Museum, das ihm gewidmet ist.

■Beckford Tower, construida en 1827 por William Beckford, tiene 156 escalones que llevan a un pequeño museo dedicado a él.

Bath's boating station.

■Jetée de Bath.

■Die Bootsstation von Bath.

■Puesto de canotaje de Bath.

The picturesque village of Newton St. Loe.

■*Le pittoresque village de Newton St. Loe.*

■*Das malerische Dorf Newton St. Loe.*

■*La pintoresca aldea de Newton St. Loe.*

The Kennet and Avon Canal at Bathampton.

■*Le Kennet & Avon Canal à Bathampton.*

■*Der Kennet-Avon-Kanal bei Bathampton.*

■*El Kennet y Avon Canal en Bathampton.*

Sleepy Widcombe tucked snugly into the hills bounding Bath.

■*Le village tranquille de Widcombe niché confortablement dans les collines délimitant Bath.*

■*Das schläfrige Widcombe schmiegt sich eng an die an Bath angrenzenden Hügel.*

■*El soñoliento Widcombe envuelto en el abrigo de las colinas que rodea Bath.*

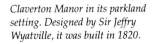

The gently rolling countryside south of the city, complete with balloons bobbing on the horizon.

■*La campagne vallonnée au sud de la ville, avec des ballons à l'horizon.*

■*Die sanft-wellige Landschaft südlich von Bath, komplett mit Ballons am Horizont.*

■*La gentil ondulada campiña al Sur de la ciudad, con globos alzándose en el horizonte y todo.*

The colonial style Boat House, now a watering hole for visitors.

■*La Boat House (hangar à bateaux) style colonial, devenu un bar pour les touristes.*

■*Das im Kolonialstil erbaute Bootshaus ist heute eine "Tränke" für Besucher.*

■*Boat House de estilo colonial, hoy en día un pub para sus visitantes.*

Bath's other watery attraction - the marina.

■*L'autre attraction aquatique de Bath - sa marina.*

■*Die andere "wässrige" Attraktion von Bath - der Jachthafen.*

■*La marina - es la otra atracción entorno a agua que se puede visitar en Bath - la marina.*

Claverton Manor in its parkland setting. Designed by Sir Jeffry Wyatville, it was built in 1820.

■*Claverton Manor dans son parc. Dessiné par Sir Jeffry Wyatville et construit en 1820.*

■*Claverton Manor inmitten seiner Parklandschaft wurde 1820 nach einem Entwurf von Sir Jeffry Wyatville erbaut.*

■*Claverton Manor se alza orgullosamente en su propio parque. Diseñado por Sir Jeffrey Wyatville, fue construido en 1820.*